Mastering Your Performance

Melanie Dreyer
University of Pittsburgh

Illustrations by Julie Allardice Ray

KENDALL/HUNT PUBLISHING COMPANY
4050 Westmark Drive Dubuque, Iowa 52002

ISBN 978-0-7575-3870-4

Printed in the United States of America
10 9 8 7 6 5 4 3 2

Introduction

Who needs to learn how to perform? The answer is we all do. In fact, everyone performs to one degree or another every day. Any time you try to control the impression you make or the message you send when you talk to someone, you are utilizing elements of performance. If you try to impress your girlfriend's parents during dinner, you are performing. If you appeal to an instructor to give you an extension on an assignment, you are performing. If you try to convince your best friend that you didn't borrow her cell phone to make that call to Japan (when in fact you did), you are performing. Many professionals use elements of performance to accomplish their goals: a lawyer performs to persuade a jury, a doctor performs to encourage a patient, a politician performs to win votes, a customer service specialist performs when fielding a complaint. The question isn't whether or not we use performance in our daily activities; the question is, how do we master our performance skills so that we may communicate what we intend and achieve our goal?

Performance skills can be broken down into components that can be practiced and mastered. Vocal inflection, facial expression, and body language are all important tools in communicating intent. Some less-obvious elements of performance include using your imagination, learning to be spontaneous, overcoming a fear of feeling foolish, understanding the message being sent by the conversation partner, and recognizing what motivates others to behave the way they do. Learning to master these skills builds self-confidence and personal charisma. Because acting is the profession most keenly devoted to mastering a performance, this book will use the tools of the stage actor to identify the various skills required for a confident performance. This book is designed to serve the student who has never studied acting but wishes to understand and learn to control his or her performance skills. All the ideas presented in this book are accomplishable by the novice performer and can be applied to multiple professions. When you have finished reading <u>Mastering Your Performance</u>, you will have a clearer understanding of the impression you make on those around you and how to modify your communication style to achieve your aim in any performance situation.

Chapter One: Letting Go

There's an old saying in the theatre: Never perform with animals or children. Why? Because their natural, relaxed behavior will steal the focus on stage. Indeed, anyone in public who appears relaxed and unselfconscious tends to draw the eye. When someone looks relaxed in public, she seems to enjoy being watched and her comfort makes it pleasurable for us to watch her. Often her gestures appear effortless and spontaneous. Her energy is specifically directed, she knows what she wants to say, and what she would like us to hear. While we listen to her, our focus shifts from her behavior to her message, almost without notice. Conversely, when someone onstage is tense and self-conscious, it becomes difficult to watch her. Her discomfort becomes our discomfort, and rather than listening to what she has to say, we become distracted by her awkward posture, strained speaking voice, and incongruent gestures. The first step in gaining this relaxed self-confidence on stage is learning to let go of fear and to find pleasure in being watched.

A. Losing Your Inhibition

When we were children, all of us were able to play spontaneously, free of self-consciousness. Children have a natural ability to become so completely involved in their activities that they forget, don't care, or perhaps even enjoy that someone is watching them. Later in life, as our behavior is more closely scrutinized, we become afraid to behave outside the social norm. We fear humiliation or being ostracized from our social group. This fear creates a chronic self-consciousness that interferes with our ability to appear relaxed and free on stage. As you begin working to overcome your inhibition, you may discover that your natural tendency is to censor yourself and to play things safe. Whenever that happens, pretend that you are four years old again, and it doesn't matter what others think. The more you can rid yourself of your fear of feeling foolish, the more relaxed you'll feel in front of other people.

B. Getting to Know Yourself

On stage actors play characters. Characters are people comprised of a series of personality traits that make them behave in a certain fashion. You are a character, as is your best friend, your mother, your boss. As individuals we are comprised of a unique array of behaviors that manifest themselves in stronger or weaker fashion, depending on the situation. You are a different person at work than you are at home. There are probably many versions of you. Every character an actor plays on stage contains a part of him. You have all of the elements you need to play any character. You are part hero, part villain, part child, part adult, part miser, part philanthropist. Think of your personality as a rainbow of possible behavior choices. When you play a role on stage, you select pieces of that rainbow and amplify them. The same technique applies to your public persona. If you give a speech at a business luncheon, you will use different aspects of your personality than when you make a guest appearance at an elementary school. Before a performer can gain control over how to use the various elements of his personality, he first needs to recognize and understand how his personality is structured.

C. Getting to Know Your Partner

Learning to really see and really listen to other people will assist you in your interpersonal communication skills both onstage and off. It is surprising how much information we can glean from a short interaction with someone if we only pay attention. Many elements come into play when picking up signals from a conversation partner.

Subliminal Information:

1. **What is she wearing?** Clothing can tell volumes about a person. She may be dressed stylishly, having taken great care to put her outfit together. She may be wearing two different colored socks. He might have on a suit, but you recognize soup stains on the tie, and that the shirt has not been properly pressed. What information does this tell you about the person in front of you? Notice the details and see how they fit into the big picture.

2. **How is he carrying himself?** Is he standing up straight and looking you right in the eye? Is he slumped and shuffling, yet doesn't seem to be tired? Does she constantly squint at you as though scrutinizing your every word? Body posture sends the strongest signal about a conversation partner's intent. Any discomfort you feel in talking with her may come from a conflict between the words you are hearing and the body language you observe. Learning to recognize and identify another's body signals can help you be prepared to respond to the unexpected.
3. **What is her tone of voice and choice of words?** Does she seem pleased and enthusiastic about your conversation? Does he sound like he'd rather watch paint dry? Does she choose her words carefully, as though trying to impress you? Does he deliberately use slang and bad language, perhaps to offend? The way a conversation partner delivers her message contains important information often overlooked by those on the receiving end.
4. **How does he respond to you?** Does he seem initially impressed only to lose interest rather quickly? Does she seem too busy to talk, but then somehow finds time to chat for twenty minutes? Which of your sentences affect your partner positively? Which seem to create tension? This dynamic of cause and effect is crucial in guiding a conversation to a positive conclusion. Unless, of course, you've decided such an outcome is no longer of interest to you.

D. Exercising your Imagination

Imagination has become an important skill in many professions. How many times have we heard "think outside the box"? Imagination is required for all forms of creative expression but is an invaluable life skill as well. Whenever you find yourself in a tricky situation (you missed your bus and have a crucial meeting in 30 minutes), an active imagination can help you find a way out. Imagination is like a muscle that can atrophy with disuse. With practice, it can come back to life and begin to serve you by offering multiple perspectives on an unlimited number of situations. At first it may seem that you were born without a creative spark. You just can't think of anything interesting to solve a problem posed to you. When you are completely stuck and cannot think of anything at all, simply relax and stop trying for a minute. Often an idea will spontaneously appear. Some people have their most creative moments in the shower or just before they go to bed. That's because the intellect is no longer censoring the imagination. Because the mind is busy with something else, new ideas are allowed to float to the surface. So the next time you get a great idea without trying, pay attention. Simply having a good idea is only part of the equation. Once the idea has made itself known to you, it is your job to act on it and not dismiss it as silly. Dismissing unexpected ideas is how the imagination muscles lose elasticity. That crazy idea you're having may be the perfect solution to the fix you're in, if only you can find the courage to act on it.

Conclusion

In this chapter, you've spent time investigating how to feel more relaxed and self-confident. Relaxation takes time and practice. Self-confidence emerges when you challenge yourself to overcome your fears and acknowledge your success. You've begun to learn how to free your inhibitions and rid yourself of the fear of feeling foolish. It is more pleasurable to experience life no longer worrying excessively about whether others find your behavior appropriate. But because you've begun learning things about yourself and how others perceive you, you can choose to modify your behavior to create a specific impression. You've begun the process of learning to listen to and understand others. Recognizing the signals others send when talking to you will help you adjust your side of a conversation so that you can achieve your goal. Really hearing what another person says — not just the words but the body language as well — is one of the most useful skills in winning someone to your side. Finally, you've begun to activate and stretch your imagination. This skill, learning to open your thinking to personal inspiration and then daring to follow through on the idea, will help you solve numerous life situations that might have seemed impossible before. In the next chapter, you'll begin learning how to warm up your body and your voice, to energize yourself in preparation for performance, and to concentrate your focus so that nothing can distract you when you are in the middle of a presentation.

Chapter Two: Good Beginnings

Just like professional athletes, actors must warm up before they are ready to play. Warming up gets the blood flowing to the body's muscles and allows greater freedom of movement. It relaxes the voice so that the actor can speak with precise volume, diction, and tone. It helps the actor to leave the day behind and focus attention on the task at hand. It can relieve stress and help alleviate nervousness. Warming up is an essential component in creating a good beginning for every rehearsal or performance.

A. Physically Warming Up

A physical warm-up gets your body ready to work. Because the body is one of the actor's primary tools, it is important to take care of it before, during, and after a performance. When physically warming up, three factors work together to prepare your body to work at maximum efficiency. To perform well, you need to be **relaxed** and free from excess tension. Your body should be **stretched and limber** so that you don't pull a muscle or tendon during physical activity. And you should be **energized** so that you can move as quickly or as slowly as your performance situation requires.

Relaxation

A relaxed physical state isn't lethargic or sleepy. It is simply stress-free and ready to respond to your commands. In life we often use far more stress and energy than required for executing certain activities. To illustrate this point, try an experiment. Watch yourself when you brush your teeth and observe how many muscles you use that you don't need (buttocks? back? neck?). Ideally, all physical activity should use only those muscles required to execute the task at hand. Anything more is wasted energy and adds stress to the body. By learning to relax on command, you can make every performance situation more enjoyable and safer for your body.

Stretching

Stretching is important to ensure that your muscles and tendons are not injured during extreme physical activity. Stretching limbers the muscles and connective tissues so that they can move with the demands of the dramatic situation. It is important to remember that stretching is both more effective and safer when your heart rate is up and the blood is pumping through your body. You'll notice that a stretch you do in the afternoon, after a day of physical activity, is easier to execute than one done first thing in the morning after hours of sleep. Always stretch at your own pace. Never try to push your body beyond its limits. A good stretch presses your muscles and tendons to the point of resistance but does not create pain. Becoming more limber takes time and patience. You will not improve your stretch within one week's time. But you will see improvement if you stretch every day for three months.

Energizing

Energizing involves getting the blood flowing in such a way that the muscles and brain are fully responsive to any movement or thought you require for your performance. When an actor is energized, she can spring onto the stage and move anywhere at a moment's notice. Her litheness and the way her body seems to vibrate with physicality are mesmerizing to watch. By contrast, an actor who isn't energized appears disinterested and lethargic. She may be nicely relaxed and limbered, but she fails to capture the eye. Her sluggish behavior is uninteresting and unattractive. Learning to energize your body will not only improve your performance in front of an audience, but it may also help you feel better as you move through your day.

B. Vocally Warming Up

Once your body has been warmed up, it is important to warm up your voice. Many vocal problems are a result of not warming up the voice before speaking. As with a physical warm-up, a vocal warm-up has multiple aspects. A good vocal warm-up starts with **breathing**, moves into using the breath to **make sounds**, and concludes with **stretching and articulation** exercises.

Breathing

As every singer knows, a good voice is supported by breathing properly. Learning to breathe in the correct manner can help you control your volume, your tone, your pitch, and your rate when talking. Most people breathe using only a small percentage of their lung capacity. Not only must an actor learn to breathe more deeply, but he must also learn to drop the breath down into the diaphragm. The diaphragm is a muscle that sits under the lungs and allows the lungs to fully expand and contract. With practice, you can learn to breathe fully and deeply, giving yourself tremendous vocal power and control.

Using Breath to Make Sound

Once you've begun learning to breathe properly, it is important to learn how to connect your breathing to your voice. Although sound originates in the throat, you should not rely on the muscles in your throat as the primary source of your voice. Anyone whose voice sounds strained or pinched is probably doing just that. People who regularly lose their voice are probably straining it through too much muscle tension in the throat. However, when the breath supports the creation of sound, the voice has enormous power and is free of strain. A tension-free voice sounds much like a well-tuned cello; a pinched voice is more like a squeaky violin.

Articulating

Deep, relaxed breathing as the foundation for speaking is part of how the actor uses her voice on stage. She must also learn how to use her lips, teeth, tongue, and jaw to clearly articulate all her lines. If you have a tendency to mumble, slur words, or say words incorrectly, articulation exercises will help you alleviate those problems. Learning to articulate is one of the most important skills an actor can learn. How can the audience get your message if they cannot understand you? Slurred speech can also send signals about laziness or poor education that you may not intend. You can even eliminate an unwanted dialect or regionalism through proper articulation.

C. Finding Focus and Energy

An actor uses more than his body and voice when performing on stage. **Focus** and **energy** play a big part in creating a mesmerizing performance. It is not uncommon to arrive for rehearsal distracted by the events of the day. It is important to learn how to leave the outside world behind and place all your attention on the task before you.

Focus

Focus is essential for accomplishing difficult intellectual tasks. Learning to focus will improve your test-taking skills, help you be a better conversation partner, and help you remember little things like names and dates that can often make a big difference when trying to create a good impression. Like every other performance skill, learning to focus takes practice. But its many benefits make it well worth the effort.

Energy

The way you hold yourself when you stand not only communicates something specific to the audience, it also dictates how energy flows through your body. It is important to find a neutral stance that is firmly connected to the ground but free and relaxed so that you can quickly and easily move to any position on stage. Actors learn to adopt an energized neutral stance from which they can move in any direction at any speed. You can experiment with this idea on your own. Adopt the casual stance of a student (weight more on one leg with a hip out, arms crossed or in pockets) and then try to walk quickly across the room as though jaywalking in heavy traffic. Try moving again, starting from a neutral stance. A body that starts moving from a neutral stance has more energy and is more responsive to the actor's needs.

D. Discovering Impulse

Impulsive behavior can be disadvantageous in many life situations. We are trained to think through our actions and be rational about major decisions whenever possible. Inspiration and creativity, however, are not born of intellectual effort but of openness to **instinct** and **impulse**. Children naturally use this ability to advantage on a daily basis. As adults, we must relearn what society has trained us to forget.

Instinct

Ever had a hunch about something? A bad feeling about a decision you were trying to make? You were probably using your instinct. Learning to honor your gut response, to listen to that little voice in your head, or to just do something because it feels right will help make your performance skills more responsive and interesting.

Impulse

Impulse defines the quick response that makes you act before the rational mind can engage. Grabbing a child's arm without thinking before she steps in front of a moving bus would be an example of how useful impulse can be. On stage, learning to use impulse is a key component to creating a dynamic performance. An actor who can follow his impulses when rehearsing will make the most discoveries when preparing a performance.

Conclusion

In this chapter you've learned the importance of physically and vocally warming up to prepare yourself to work. A physical warm-up helps you relax and release unwanted tension, limbers you up so that you can keep your body safe, and energizes you so that you can give a dynamic performance. A vocal warm-up reminds you to breathe deeply, to use your breath to create sound, and to activate your mouth so that you can articulate clearly. Additionally, you've explored the value of focusing your mind so that unwanted experiences don't color your performance. You've begun to work with a neutral stance that maximizes the flow of energy, allowing your body to respond quickly. Finally, you've begun to reawaken your imagination and your impulse, recognizing the value in learning to respond instinctively when performing on stage. In the next chapter, you will begin to extend the idea of using your body, voice, and imagination when you perform and to identify how you can use each to clearly communicate ideas.

Chapter Three: The Actor's Instrument

All artists use a medium to communicate their message. The visual artist uses paints and canvas, the sculptor may create with clay or steel, the musician plays on an instrument. The actor's medium is the voice and the body. Now that you've begun to get a sense of how the various elements of your acting instrument work, you can learn how to use them to communicate specific ideas. In this chapter you will start by isolating the use of your body and your voice to give you a sense of the possibilities of each in conveying meaning.

A. Using the Voice to Communicate Ideas

Your voice is comprised of multiple characteristics, all of which can be manipulated or modified when you want to communicate something specific. You can modulate your **tone**, making it harsh, soft, strident, soothing, full, or weak. You can control your **volume** to result in anything between whispering and shouting. You can determine your **diction**, mumbling to convey shyness or hesitance, overarticulating to indicate superiority or snobbishness, or a mixture to suggest you come from a certain social class or part of the country. You can even learn various **dialects** should you want to pretend to be from another land or region.

<u>Tone</u>

Tone controls the quality of the sound of your voice. For normal speaking, you will probably want a pleasant, open tone that suggests you are happy and relaxed. Some characters and emotional situations are better expressed with a more extreme choice. You may want a strident, harsh tone for a villainess, a soft, weak tone when playing someone on his deathbed, a bouncy, energized tone if you are playing a child. Become aware of how tone functions as you use your voice, and you will have one of the keys to distinguishing one character from another.

Volume

Volume controls how loudly or softly you speak. It is important to recognize whether or not you speak with appropriate volume in any situation. Volume not only helps the listener understand the words you say, it also is a key component in conveying confidence when you speak. Those who speak in a soft, shy voice suggest that what they have to say is not important. Those who speak too loudly can appear to be boorish.

Diction

Diction involves both articulation and word choice. Moving your jaw, lips, teeth, and tongue so that you can effectively execute the sounds required of speech is part of the challenge of being understood. You must also choose words that make sense both in their construction and their context. You wouldn't use the same turns of phrase to talk with a customs official at the airport as you would with a friend at a bar. On stage, diction can be manipulated to help convey character. Too much diction might suggest a snob. Too little diction might make your character sound drunk.

Dialects

A dialect can be a wonderful element of character interpretation. On the other hand, unwanted dialects can create a problem. Aspiring television journalists must eliminate that Southern drawl or their Brooklynese. Any voice specialist can help you diagnose and remove an unwanted dialect should you wish to adopt a more neutral sound.

B. Using the Body to Communicate Ideas

Spend some time watching people at the supermarket or the bus stop. Do you make assumptions about who they are based on how they carry themselves? Can you tell if someone is having a bad day? If he is overly tired or stressed? If he seems to have just fallen in love? How do you know those things might be true if you've never spoken with him? Your **posture**, your **gestures**, your **facial expressions**, your **pace and rhythm** when you walk or sit, all these things are controllable elements of your communication style. Additionally, the **environment** in which you are situated can greatly affect the body language you use.

Posture

Posture immediately communicates information to the viewer. A relaxed posture suggests a different kind of person than a rigid posture might. An actor can communicate a character's age through posture. Where your head is placed, where your shoulders sit, how your arms hang, how your torso lines up, how you stand on your legs are all components of posture that can be controlled by you.

Gestures

Do you know people who speak with their hands? Someone who always plays with her hair? Who chronically bites a pencil? These are all gestures that convey character information. Relaxed gestures that fit the conversation are the ideal when you are yourself and not playing a character in a scene. A character you play may have telltale quirks in his behavior that are expressed through certain kinds of gestures. Learning to identify how you may be using gesture inappropriately gives you the opportunity to replace unwanted behavior with gestures that convey the impression you intend.

Facial Expressions

It is helpful to know how much you use your face when expressing an idea. Some people have a mask that covers all expression of feeling. Others seem overly active as they engage in conversation, constantly lifting eyebrows, smiling excessively, or frowning inappropriately. The right facial expression is important in helping the audience understand what you mean when you speak. Sometimes the words a character says don't match the intent. When she says, "I forgive you," and doesn't sound like she really means it, it is often the facial expression that creates the disparity.

Pace and Rhythm

Everyone has a natural metabolism. Some people have a high metabolism and seem to never sit still. Others have a low metabolism and seem to move as though under water. Pace identifies how quickly or slowly you move. Rhythm refers to the way your movement is divided across time. If you move erratically, with no particular pattern, your rhythm might resemble a jazz riff. If you move with steady precision, your rhythm might resemble a drum beat. Rhythm can be paired with pace in almost any combination to create the details of how a character moves.

Environments

The way a person moves and speaks can tell us much about who he is. Where a person is located can also have a strong effect on behavior. If we observed a person while walking through a park at midday, he would carry himself differently than if he were walking down a dark alley at night. The environment in which a character is situated often influences how that character behaves both negatively and positively.

Conclusion

In this chapter you've had the opportunity to explore how the body and voice convey information about who you are to the world around you. As you become more aware of the details of your behavior, you will learn to control how you are seen by others. In the theatre, actors use the body and voice to distinguish one character from another. You are now ready to begin learning how to perform a dramatic situation provided by a playwright. Chapter Four will give you the tools you need understand how the story of a play is constructed, and how you can investigate that story to find the information you need to build a character.

Chapter Four: Unlocking Dramatic Structure

Now that you've begun to get a sense of how your body, mind and imagination work in conveying information to others, it's time to examine how this process works in a play. To an audience member, a play is a story brought to life by actors on a stage. They come to the theatre, sit in their seats, and await the opportunity to be delighted by the tale. To the actor, a play is a world unto itself, filled with information that guides and directs everyone involved in telling the story. Unlike a novel, a play does not explain every detail. Often the information an actor requires to understand the character may be buried in a stage direction, in another character's dialogue, or in something that someone references in another scene. Because a play contains so much compact information, it is important for an actor to learn how to read it carefully. Careful reading will provide the knowledge necessary for understanding a character's behavior. An actor reads a play as a detective might, constantly searching for clues that will inform him about the person he is playing.

A. How to Read a Play

You will need to read any play more than once to truly understand how it works. It takes two to three hours to read the average play. Plan to read the play *at least* four times in the course of creating a character. Professional actors often read a play a dozen times during the rehearsal process.

<u>The First and Second Readings</u>

The **first time** you read a play is special. If you are unfamiliar with the story, your first experience with the play will be the most similar to what you might experience as an audience member. You can never recapture that sense of innocence and surprise. If possible, read the play the first time through all in one sitting, undisturbed by intrusions and interruptions. Additionally, have a pencil handy and make notes in the margins of the script (if it is yours) or in a notebook. Identify any moments in the story that strongly affect you.

The **second time** you read the play plan to gather information. Although you already know the story, you will recognize many details that you missed the first time. Circle anything that seems important. Feel free to flip back and forth, cross-referencing different sections. In your second read of the play, you begin the process of analysis that is important in preparing your role.

B. Identifying Structure

It is important for an actor to recognize how a play has been structured by the playwright to achieve a specific effect. The events in the play are told in a deliberate order. Your job is to understand how the individual elements of the story fit together to weave the tale. Most plays are written using a traditional narrative, with a beginning that provides background for the story, a middle that offers some sort of problem or crisis, and an end in which the crisis is resolved. This traditional model has the following elements:

<u>The Problem</u>
Every play has a problem around which the story is centered. Identifying the problem is the first step to understanding how the structure of the play illuminates this conflict and its resolution.

<u>Initial Event</u>
This is the event that initiates the problem in the play. The story is free from complication before this event. What one thing begins it all? Where does the problem start?

<u>Complicating Actions</u>
These events continue to make the problem worse, placing more and more pressure on the situation. There are often several of them, each building on the others.

<u>Climax</u>
The moment where the crisis is at its worst. The problem is at its peak. The emotional intensity for the characters and the audience is at its height.

Resolution

Once the climax is over, the world of the play begins to right itself. The resolution often contains the aftermath of the crisis presented in the play.

C. How to Watch a Play

In addition to the exercise work you do in the classroom, watching a play in performance will inform you about what works on stage and what does not. Usually you will witness the work of actors who have more experience than you do. You can see firsthand where their acting convinces you of what they are saying and where it falls short. You can use the live theatre experience to identify how to modify your own performance technique, to model successful behavior, and to avoid choices that fail to persuade.

Going to the theatre is different from going to the movies. There is theatre etiquette one must follow to ensure the comfort of the audience and that of the actors. Here is a list of rules that are considered standard protocol.

Rules for Attending Live Theatre:

1. **Arrive early**. Those who arrive late disrupt everyone's experience. Not only does the audience have to deal with making room for you to take your seat while they are trying to watch the show, but also the actors notice that you've arrived late, and it interferes with their concentration.
2. **No talking during the performance**. It is rude to talk during a film as well, but talking is more harmful during a live performance. The actors can hear you when you whisper to your friend. It is distracting for those watching and for those performing. Save your conversation for intermission or after the show.
3. **No eating or drinking in the theatre**. Snacks are a wonderful part of the experience of going to a film. However, no one is allowed to eat or drink during a play. This is partly because such behavior would be distracting to the actors, but it is primarily because a theatre is not designed to endure the mess food and drink can make. You can often purchase snacks and drinks at intermission if you find you are hungry or thirsty, but you must eat them in lobby.

4. **Turn off your cell phone.** Talking during a performance is distracting but the ring of a cell phone completely breaks the illusion the actors are trying to create on stage. If your phone rings, it will annoy everyone in the theatre and embarrass you. Don't forget to turn it off.
5. **Don't take notes during the show.** During a live performance, the actors are constantly aware of what the audience is doing and how they are feeling. It is part of the actors' job to pay attention to those who have come to see them perform. It is distracting to the actors to see audience members scribbling in a notebook when they should be watching the performance. Even critics are aware of this and bring only small notebooks in which they write a few notes on the sly to keep their distracting behavior to a minimum.
6. **Use the restroom at intermission.** Unless it is an emergency, wait to use the facilities until intermission or after the show. If you must go and cannot wait, most people will understand, but they won't be happy about the disturbance during the performance.
7. **Stay for the entire show.** Even if you don't like the play, remember that you are there to learn from observing, not just to be entertained. You can learn a lot from what isn't working, and the second act may surprise you. You cannot see how the actors are crafting their entire performance if you don't stay for the whole thing.

For the acting student who is coming to see a play for class, it is helpful to prepare ahead of time to get the most from the viewing experience. The following may assist you in preparing to watch a play for the purpose of analyzing performance technique.

<u>Watching a Play from a Critical Perspective:</u>

1. If possible, **read** the play you will see **ahead** of time and discuss the content as a class.
2. On the evening of the play, **arrive** at the theatre at least **fifteen minutes early** and take your seat.
3. Before the play begins, **observe the setting** on the stage and take note of the atmosphere that has been created. Is it a realistic set (a room, a yard) or a nonrealistic set (abstract in design)? What kind of people will inhabit this space? Can you imagine how this environment will affect the characters' behavior? Does it look like the world you imagined when you read the play?

4. **Read your program.** Read the director's notes, dramaturgical articles and any other extra information about the play. Read the actors' biographies and note how much experience each actor brings to the part. Choose two of the characters in the play whose performances you will follow and note which actors play them.
5. During the first act of the play, **pay** particular **attention to the characters** you've chosen. Do you believe what they are saying? If so, what makes them credible? Do you find their behavior false? What is the actor doing that fails to convince you? Find a couple of specific moments that stayed with you as positive or negative.
6. At intermission **make notes** on what you saw.
7. Perform the same critical observation process during Act 2. When the play is over, note for yourself whether or not you were satisfied with the two performances you observed. Did you see behavior you could model when you create your own character for class? Did they make mistakes you'd like to avoid? Write your observations down for later use in your performance review.

Conclusion

This chapter has given you the opportunity to examine a play by analyzing its structure and by watching other performers tell the story. In order to prepare a role, the actor must be able to understand dramatic structure and how her character fits into the greater whole of the story line. Therefore, it is important to learn how to read a play from the actor's perspective. Going to the theatre is one of the best ways to learn about acting. Watching more experienced actors perform will allow you to see your classroom lessons in practice and offer you the opportunity to develop a critical eye for what works and what doesn't in any given performance. The next chapter will add to your arsenal by introducing you to the theatre terminology you will need when working on a scene.

Chapter Five: Theatre Lingo

As with every profession, the theatre has its own special language. There are theatres of various types in which an actor might be asked to play, each requiring the actor to adjust the performance to fit the space. There are special names for the architectural elements of the theatre, which are regularly referenced in rehearsal and production. There are even names for the tasks involved in creating a play, specifically the language used to determine how the actor moves on the stage, without which it would be difficult for the director and actor to communicate. It is helpful to learn some of this industry-specific vocabulary before beginning work on your first scene.

A. Theatre Types

There are many types of theatres where one might stage a play. Each has unique characteristics that determine the actor/audience relationship.

<u>Proscenium Theatre:</u>
A proscenium theatre contains an architectural element called a proscenium arch. This arch surrounds the opening of the stage through which the audience views the play. The proscenium arch functions as a kind of picture frame for the action of the story. In many realistic plays this frame provides what is called the "fourth wall" of the theatre. If the play takes place in a living room, for example, the audience would be viewing the action through one of the four walls of that space, as though eavesdropping on the lives of the characters. The auditoriums for proscenium theatres can range in size from 50 to 5,000 seats. In this space, actors must endeavor to face the audience as much as possible. Additionally they must play with enough volume and physical energy that even the very last row of the balcony can hear them and understand their behavior. Many proscenium theatres have fly systems, a large open space above the stage where scenery, lighting booms, or actors may be "flown" up and

down either in view of the audience or behind a curtain. Scenic elements can appear and disappear within a matter of seconds. Proscenium theatres are ideal for large productions that require space and size to achieve their artistic aims.

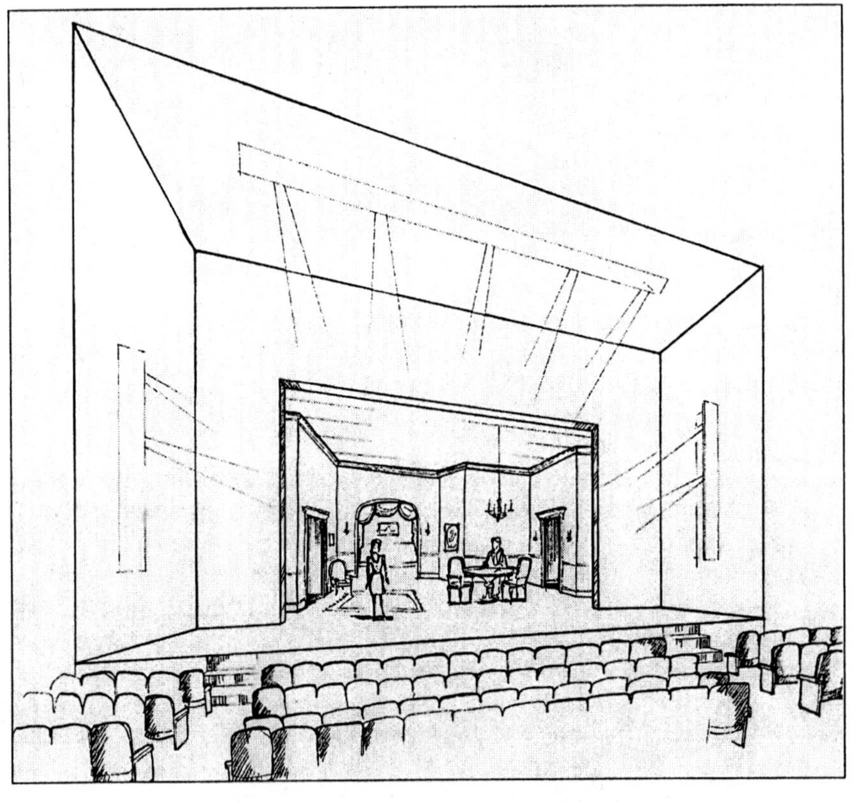

Proscenium Theatre

Thrust Theatre:

The thrust theatre wraps the auditorium around the stage, thereby increasing the level of intimacy with the audience. This wrap around element gives the stage the appearance of "thrusting" out into the audience. In this configuration, the actors are closer to the audience members, allowing patrons to view the action in more detail. Because a large portion of stage is in the auditorium, the scenery must be planned carefully so that it doesn't block the view for some of the audience members. Actors must adjust their playing style, using angled body positions to allow as many audience members as possible to see them.

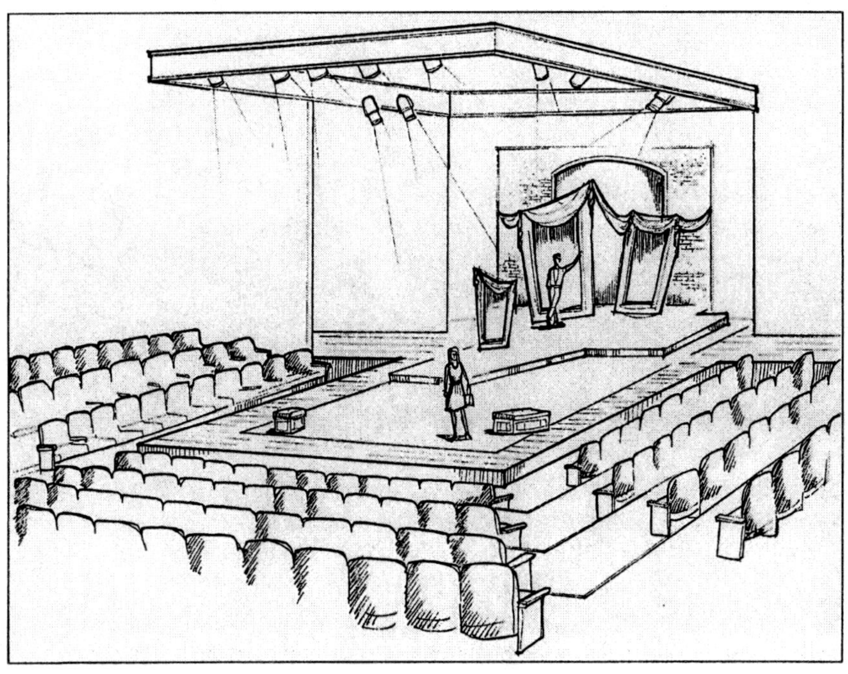

Thrust Theatre

Arena Theatre:

The arena theatre contains a playing space in the center with the audience on all four sides. This configuration is the most intimate experience for the actors and the audience members. In arena theatre, the actors always play in full view of the audience regardless of where they stand. The set designers must take care to use furniture that is low enough to prevent viewing problems for audience members. In an arena theatre, the actors do not need to worry about body position. However, because they always have their back to someone, they must take care to speak loudly and clearly.

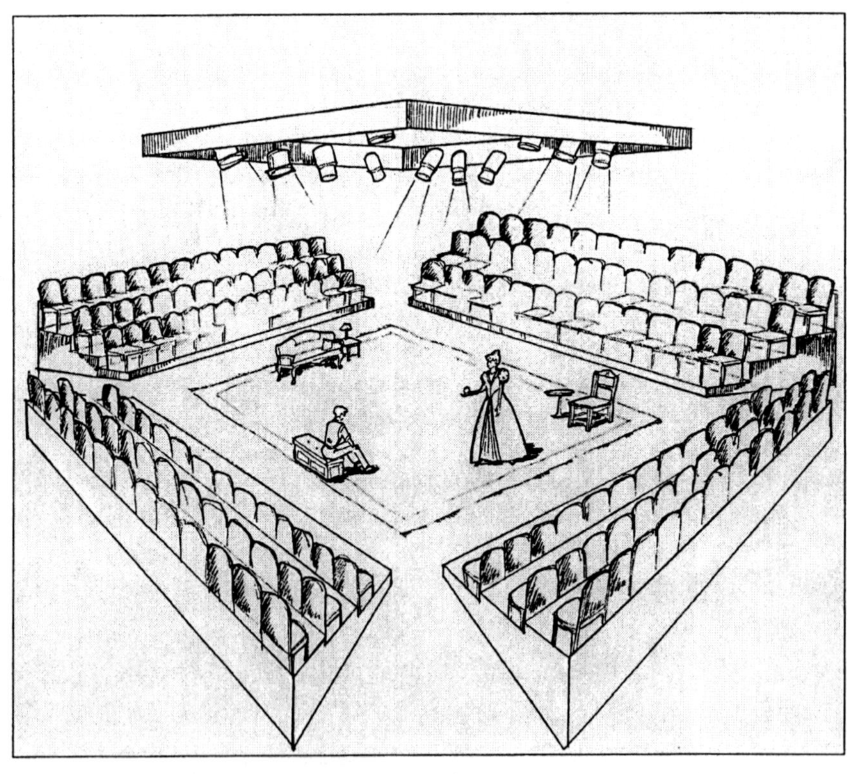

Arena Theatre

Black Box Theatre:

The black box theatre refers to a theatre space that is flexible enough to be configured in numerous ways. With the use of portable seating platforms, the space can be set up as proscenium, thrust, or arena, the specifics determined by the director and the needs of the production. A black box also creates an intimate experience for the audience and is the theatre of choice for many experimental theatre companies. Because of its size, most black box theatres cannot seat large crowds. In fact, the number of seats available to patrons will depend on the configuration of the seating platforms and their relationship to the playing space. For that reason, actors must be flexible in their playing style and respond to the needs of the current production's design.

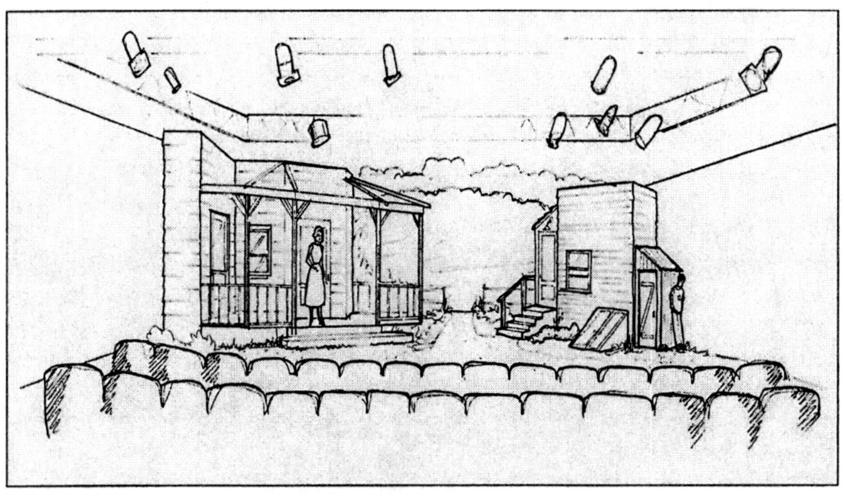

Black Box Theatre in a Proscenium Configuration

Amphitheater:

An amphitheater is an outdoor theatre often containing a seating area built into a hillside with the playing area situated at the bottom of the hill. Amphitheaters are most commonly used by theatres that play during the summer months. Outdoor theatre can be a fun experience for the audience and the actors, but it is fraught with obstacles. The weather, insects, and amplification can create problems. In an amphitheatre, actors must speak quite loudly and clearly in order to be heard because of the acoustic interference of the surrounding area.

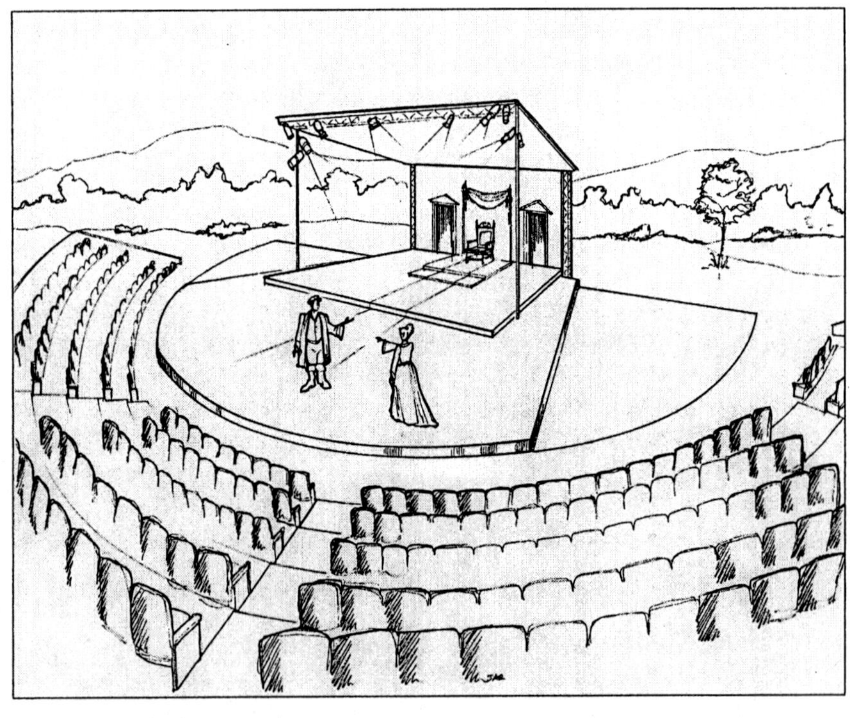

Amphitheatre

Site-Specific Theatre:
Site-specific theatre uses a space that is not a traditional theatre, but that will somehow illuminate the experience for the audience. Setting a play based on the Chicago meatpacking industry in a former slaughterhouse, for example, might help bring that experience to life. Site-specific theatre is an exciting adventure for many theatre patrons, but can be a **challenging experience. Toilet facilities may be portable johns,** the seating area may be difficult or uncomfortable, and it may be hard to find the location where the play is being held. Often the effort is worth it. Site-specific theatre, when done well, can create a memorable theatre experience. Actors must be adaptable under these conditions, varying the size of their playing style to the particular requirements of the space.

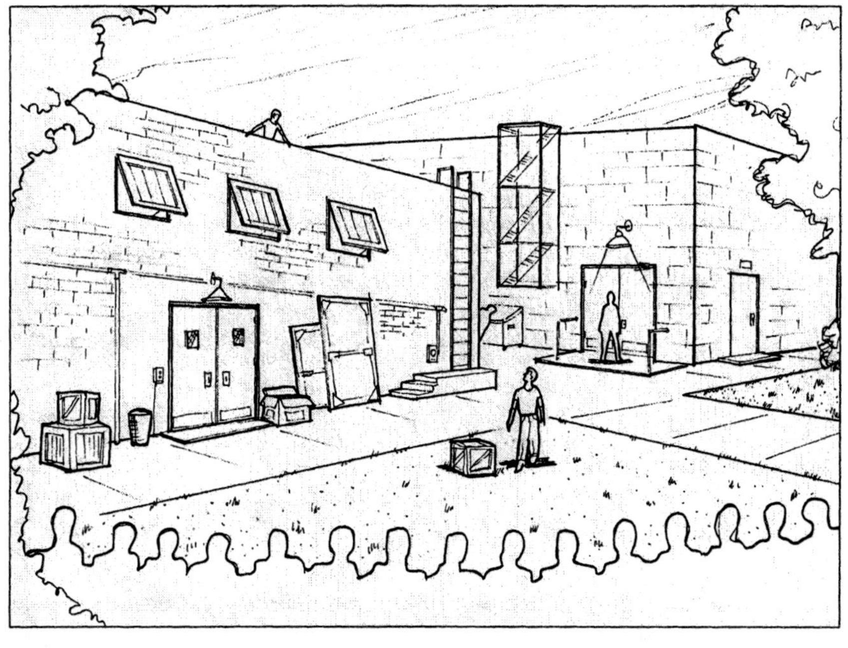

Site-Specific Theatre

B. Theatre Architecture

Here are some architectural elements specific to the theatre that you will need to know:

Architectural Elements

Apron: In a proscenium theatre, the area of the stage in front of the curtain line, closest to the audience.

Curtain Line: The line on the stage where the curtain lives in its down position.

Dressing Room: The place where the actors put on costumes and makeup.

Fourth Wall: The imaginary wall that separates the actors from the audience.

Fly Space: The large space above a proscenium stage where scenery or lighting instruments may be stored out of sight and then lowered down onto the stage for use during the production.

Green Room: Where the actors wait until they are ready to go onstage.

House: Where the audience sits.

Proscenium Arch: The archway around the opening of the stage space, which forms a picture frame through which the audience views the play.

Trap: A hole in the stage floor through which actors, props, or scenic elements may disappear as if by magic.

Vom: Short for vomitorium. A pathway through the audience that the actors use to enter or exit. Commonly used in the thrust theatre configuration.

Wings: The area just offstage where actors wait to enter onto the stage.

C. Stage Geography

Every stage contains identifiable areas that help the actors know where they are supposed to move in the play. Because the director often gives the actor her moves, the actor and director need a common language that will help them communicate during this process.

Upstage/Downstage

If you think of the stage as a big map, upstage and downstage identify those parts of the map that correspond to north and south. Upstage is north or away from the audience, downstage is south or toward the audience. These designations come from a time when the stage was raked or tipped with the north end higher than the south end to allow the audience a better view of the action on stage. At that time, upstage was literally higher up in the air than downstage. Today this viewing problem is often solved by raking the auditorium rather than the stage.

Stage Left/Right

Left and right are self explanatory in terms of direction. The important element to note is that these directions are from the actor's perspective, not that of the audience. When an actor moves stage left or east on the stage, it appears to the audience that he is moving right. Stage right is the area corresponding to the west on our map.

Stage Center

Center stage is the most central point from all edges of the stage. There are also center points in each of the four areas named above. Downstage center is the center position furthest downstage. Upstage center is its opposite. Stage left center is the center point from north to south at the left side of the stage. And stage right center corresponds to the same idea on the other side.

Other Combinations

All of the areas listed above may be combined for precision in communicating exactly where the actor should move. Downstage left, for example, suggests moving to the area downstage and left of center. Downstage left center, however, identifies that place that is equidistant between downstage center and downstage left.

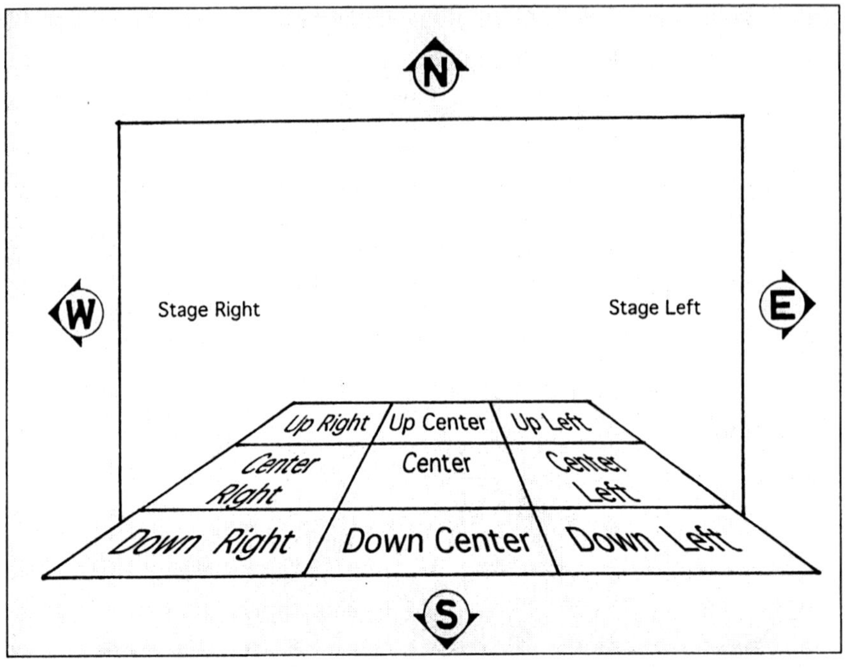

D. The Actor's Movements

The actor's movement in a play is called *blocking.* Blocking is often provided by the director who will inform the actor where to move using the vocabulary described earlier. A few other terms are often employed in the theatre, which will be useful to learn.

The Actor's Terminology

Ad Lib: To make up dialogue or business on stage. Often employed in an emergency when another actor forgets lines or entrances.

Blocking: The actor's movements, often given by the director.

Cheating: Turning oneself toward the audience so that more of the body is visible to the spectators.

Closed Position: A stage position that closes the body off from the audience's view. In a closed position, the actor is often facing more upstage than downstage.
Cross: To move from one position on the stage to another.
Countercross: To cross simultaneously with another actor, often in an opposite or counterdirection, to maximize focus and composition.
Cue: The signal to begin speaking. Often the end of the other actor's line, but could include the end of some stage business, sound effect, or lighting moment.
Curved Cross: A cross that does not follow a straight line but rather curves from point A to point B.
Curtain Call: The actors' bows at the end of the show.
Full Front/Back: A stage position in which the actor is positioned with her front or her back fully in view of the audience, employing no angles whatsoever.
Off-Book: When an actor has memorized the lines and no longer has to hold the text or "book" in order to play.
Open Position: A stage position that opens the body up to the audience's view. In an open position, the actor is often facing more downstage than upstage.
Pick Up Cues: A process of eliminating the pause between one actor's line and another's.
Property (Prop): Any item used in the play that is not costumes or furniture. For example, a carafe with wine, cigarettes, a gun, pen and paper.
Prop Table: Where props are stored backstage so that the actor can easily find them before entering to play the scene.
Stage Business: Any business that occurs on stage, often involving props. For example: pouring a drink, smoking a cigarette, cleaning a gun, writing a letter.
Upstaging: Can reference two meanings. 1. When an actor is positioned upstage in such a way that it obligates the other actor to turn his back to the audience. 2. When an actor engages in behavior that draws the focus of the audience away from the central scene. Both are considered inappropriate and undesirable behavior.

E. Recording Blocking

It is important to write down every move the director gives you when rehearsing a play. The stage manager will do this as well, but there are times when the stage manager isn't fast enough to record everything. The actor is responsible for remembering the moves learned in rehearsal, and the easiest way to do that is to *write it down.* Plan to come to every rehearsal with a pencil and a good eraser. Here are some common symbols you can use as shorthand when recording your blocking.

Blocking Shorthand
Cross = X
Upstage = US
Downstage = DS
Stage right = SR
Stage left = SL

All other terms are up to you. Some actors create their own shorthand. CX for Countercross or ~X for Curved Cross. You can use any code you like as long as you can understand it later.

Conclusion

In this chapter you've begun to learn some of the industry-specific language you will need when working on a character in a scene or a production. Theatres come in many shapes and sizes, and the actor must adapt her playing style accordingly. The director and the actor require a method by which they may easily communicate when determining blocking. Specific names for stage areas, as well as the other terms provided in this chapter, facilitate the process of learning the moves on stage. Memorizing terms is unnecessary. The words you need to know will be used regularly, and you will learn them naturally as a part of the process. Feel free to return to this chapter whenever the use of a new word arises.

Chapter Six: Given Circumstances

Given circumstances is the term used to define all the information in the play that determines who your character is and why he does what he does. Much of the information you need for character analysis will be provided by the playwright, but not all. Some of the details you must manufacture from your imagination as you prepare your scene. You will also make discoveries during rehearsal. Your job as actor is to understand as much as possible about the character in the play and then convey those circumstances in a believable way to the audience. You are charged with telling this character's tale, and you need to know who they are before you begin. The place to begin gathering information is in the text of the play.

Think of the given circumstances as the four "W"s: *Who, What, Where,* and *When.* Although Why is often included in this list, we'll be addressing both Why and How in the next chapter. Before approaching a full play, we will begin applying given circumstances to an open scene. This will require more imagination than detective work because an open scene is designed to allow you to fill in the blanks. But through this exercise you will begin to understand how given circumstances affect everything you do on stage.

A. When

You began working on the When of the play during chapter four when you were examining the play's structure. Now we will look at the When of the play in more detail. Here are some helpful questions for determining the When of your character.

Determining When

1. In what year does the action take place? What significance does this date have for your character?
2. What season is it? Does this dictate how your character feels, what they wear, what they do?

3. What day of the week is it? Over what span of time does the play take place? Does the day of week hold significance?
4. What time of day is it? How is that important? Does the time change?

B. Where

Where the play takes place will affect what your setting will look like, what furniture you will use, what kind of atmosphere you will try to create with your surroundings. Additionally, the Where should affect your character in a specific way. How your character feels about the environment in which the play takes place has an important influence on her behavior.

Determining Where

1. Where geographically does the play take place? What is significant about this location in general and specifically for your character?
2. Where logistically does the play take place? Is it inside or outside? Is it sunny or dark? Is it a place filled with things or is it relatively empty? What about this location is significant for your character?
3. Does the Where change over the course of the play? Whether yes or no, what information does that give you about playing the character?

You will have to use classroom furniture and a lot of imagination to recreate the setting of the play for your scene. A setting for a play on stage will never look exactly like the same environment might in reality. In the theatre, we often have to adjust playing environments to allow the audience to see more of the action. In your living room, for example, you might place the sofa and armchairs against the wall. On stage it is often more useful to leave space around them so that actors have more places to go. The following guidelines may help you as you convert your understanding of the scene's environment to the world of the theatre.

Helpful Hints for Creating a Playable Set

- Position the furniture pieces in such a way that the characters can move in and around them.
- Use angles whenever possible. Angles are more interesting to view than straight lines.

- Create at least **three** playing spaces so that the characters have somewhere to go. A playing space might be a sofa and chair, a credenza with drinks, a desk with papers, a bus stop.
- Use depth as well as width. Place furniture both upstage and as well as down in the corners.

C. Who

Who you are as your character can be as complex as who you are yourself. During our explorations in chapter one you began to discover things about yourself. You must now apply your awareness of human nature to an understanding of who your character is and why they do the things they do. This process of discovering the Who of your character is continuous and evolving. It will be ongoing even through your final performance. The following questions will begin your journey into understanding the particulars of your character's nature.

Determining Who

1. How old are you? Is this important to you?
2. Where are you from originally, and how do you feel about it?
3. What do you do for a living? Do you like it? Did you go to school for it? What would you be doing if your dream came true?
4. What is your socioeconomic status? Are you rich or poor? Have you always been so? Do you always want to be?
5. Are you religious?
6. Who are your parents, and what is your relationship with them?
7. Do you have siblings? Do you get along with them?
8. What are the values that are most important to you?
9. Do you have any hobbies or eccentricities?
10. What is your logistical and emotional relationship with each of the other characters in the play? Include any important characters that are referenced in the play or scene.

D. What

Every play has a problem. Every character has a crisis that references that problem. Once you've identified the play's problem, you will find your character's relationship to it. For example, let's say the play's problem is that your parents just lost all their money in the stock market. You've been accepted to Harvard, and you dream of becoming a surgeon. Your parents can no longer afford to send you to medical school. Your parents' problem directly affects your desires and creates a crisis for you in the play. To help you find the crisis in your play or scene, answer the following questions about your play.

Determining What

1. What is the play's central problem?
2. How does this problem affect your character? Does it stand in the way of something you desire?
3. Does your character try to work around the problem? How?
4. What obstacles does your character encounter?
5. Where does the scene you are performing fit into this journey?

Conclusion

Given circumstances provide the foundation on which an actor creates a character. The more you know about the play, the more you will know about the world in which your character lives, where your character came from, what she wants the most, who she loves, and who she hates. Think of the process of finding the given circumstances as a treasure hunt. Each time you read the play, you will discover something new that you hadn't seen before, which will inform you about your character. Although it takes time to map out the world of the play, it is worth the effort. You will more easily understand why your character says what she says and does what she does when you understand the world in which she makes those choices. Once you've mapped out the given circumstances for your play, you are ready to move on to playing the scene.

Chapter Seven: Putting the Story into Action

When looking at the lines in a play, most young actors will ask themselves, "How am I supposed to say these words? Should I be loud or soft? Fast or slow? Nasty or nice?" These are all legitimate questions, but thinking of how to say a line will ultimately lead to a wooden performance that is uninteresting to watch. When determining how a character might speak the words, rather than thinking about how to say the line, it is important to focus on what your character wants, how he will go about getting it and what stands in the way of achieving that goal. This trio of attributes (the *want*, the *means*, the *things to overcome*) is called **objectives**, **actions**, and **obstacles**. Objectives, actions, and obstacles, when used together to prepare a role create a map of behavior for the character. This map determines how a character behaves while making active choices to achieve his goal, and how he responds to what the other characters are doing onstage. This acting map of objectives, actions, and obstacles is called a **unit breakdown**. The unit breakdown divides the lines of the play into smaller sections or **units of action**, each section devoted to a character's objective. This creates a clear guideline for the actor when making choices about a character's behavior. Although these words may seem foreign at first (objective, action, obstacle, unit breakdown, units of action), you will soon discover that they provide the key to learning how to say the line by fighting for what the character wants, rather than making contrived decisions about how to speak or move.

A. The Objective: Not How But Why

The objective is defined as the character's need or want. Every character has something she wants at every moment of the play. Sometimes what the character wants will remain the same for several pages of the text. Sometimes what she wants will change several times within that same period.

Finding the character's objective is the first step to figuring out what to do onstage. Don't focus on how to say the line, focus on why your character needs to say it. Let's return to our example of the young person who dreams of going to Harvard but whose parents just lost all their money in a stock market crash. The scene you will play takes place in the living room one hour after the news of the crash. The dialogue directs you to enter the room and begin asking questions about the event. How will you say those lines? First let's determine why you ask these questions. Perhaps you recognize your parents' misery and want *to find a way to comfort them.* Perhaps you have an appointment with a friend and want *to assuage your own guilty conscience* before you leave for your date. Or perhaps you want *to find out how much money will be left for your college tuition at Harvard.* Any of these three objectives might work for the scene. Each will change the way you behave, and the decision is an important one for telling the character's story.

B. The Action: How Do I Get What I Want?

The objective tells the actor *why* he says the line, but it is the action that gives him the possibilities of *how.* An action is a verb, relating to an objective, which provides the tactic the character uses to achieve his aim. Using our earlier example, let's say you want *to find out how much money will be left for your college tuition at Harvard.* Your objective is clear. How you will achieve it is determined by your action. Will you probe your parents to tell you? Demand that they do so? Hint around? Ask directly? Coax the information from them? The possibilities are numerous. The words the playwright gives the character often suggest a range of playable actions that fit the character's intent. In rehearsal, the actor can try many verbs as he endeavors to get what he wants. During this process of trial and error he may discover what works best for the character at a particular moment in the play. When choosing actions, always use active verbs that may encounter resistance from the other character. To "explain" or "convince" is a possible choice but a dull one. To "persuade" or "press" is more interesting to play.

C. The Obstacle: What Stands in My Way?

Objectives determine *why* you say your line. Actions determine *how* you say your line. But it is the obstacle that makes a performance interesting. Obstacles are what add dramatic tension to any story. Imagine if Romeo asked for Juliet's hand in marriage and got it without question. It makes a pretty dull story. If he must disguise himself to meet her, visit her in secret, suffer banishment from his friends and family, and then discover her dead when they finally reunite, it makes the story more exciting. So to add interest to your performance, it is important to determine those things that stand in the way of your character's goal. Think of obstacles as falling into two categories: internal and external.

<u>Internal Obstacle</u>
An internal obstacle is something within the makeup of the character that stands in the way. Perhaps Romeo doesn't believe himself worthy of Juliet or has a fear of ghosts and can't bring himself to meet her at the tomb.

<u>External Obstacle</u>
An external obstacle comes from forces outside the makeup of the character, a circumstance that isn't generated by the character's personality or psychology. Romeo's family hates Juliet's family, preventing him from seeing her; he is taunted into killing Juliet's cousin and is then banished from his home; he doesn't get the message that Juliet isn't really dead and kills himself to be with her. Finding the obstacles is the third step in creating your unit breakdown.

D. Units of Action

A unit of action is the playing time from one objective to the next. The unit breakdown divides the script into units of action, one following another, each with its own set of objectives, actions, and obstacles. Actors use the units of action to determine the character's story. A character in a play always wants something or is always in the process of trying to achieve an objective. Each section of text that is dedicated to a specific objective comprises one unit of action. The actor can then map out the character's journey into units of action, one after another. Remember that each unit of action contains one objective, multiple actions, and internal and external obstacles. It looks like this:

1 unit of action = 1 objective + many verbs + several obstacles.

It is helpful to map these units out in your script. Begin by drawing a line across the page where a new objective begins. Using the text from an open scene, it might look like this:

The scene you are given:

A: Oh, excuse me.
B: Oh, excuse me.
A: I'm sorry.
B: It's okay. I'm sorry.
A: What?
B: Nothing.
A: Oh.
B: Hand me that, would you?
A: This?
B: Yeah.
A: It's not yours.
A: Well, alright.
B: Thank you.
A: Really, I didn't think...
B: Sssh.
A: Oh.
B: Sorry, what was that?
A: Nothing.
B: No.

Your Unit Breakdown:

(determined with partner)
Place: Movie Theatre
Time: 7:30pm
Relationship: Strangers

Character you are playing = B

(determined on your own)

Objective 1:	To watch the movie.
Ext. Obstacle:	The other character is trying to get to her seat.

Int. Obstacle:	You are full of excitement and anxiety about seeing your favorite movie star in this film.

A:	Oh, excuse me.	
B:	Oh, excuse me.	*by apologizing* (these are the actions)
A:	I'm sorry.	
B:	It's okay. I'm sorry.	*by shutting her up*
A:	What?	
B:	Nothing.	*by dismissing her*
A:	Oh.	

Objective 2:	To get something to eat.
Ext. Obstacle:	I don't have any money, the other character doesn't want me to steal someone's popcorn.
Int. Obstacle:	None.

B: Hand me that, would you? *by conspiring*

(referring to a box of popcorn left behind by another patron who is using the bathroom)

A:	This?	
B:	Yeah.	*by affirming*
A:	It's not yours.	
B:	Hand it to me.	*by insisting*
A:	Well, alright.	
B:	Thank you.	*by offering gratitude*
A:	Really, I didn't think...	

Objective 3:	To get back to my movie.
Ext. Obstacle:	The other character is staring at me.
Int. Obstacle:	I feel bad for being rude to her.

B:	Sssh.	*by hissing*
A:	Oh.	
B:	Sorry, what was that?	*by making up*
A:	Nothing.	
B:	No.	*by regretting*

This map presents only one set of possibilities for given circumstances, objectives, actions, and obstacles. You can see as you examine it that the story unfolds as follows: "B" wants to watch the newest movie starring her favorite actor. "A" interrupts a really good part revealing the popcorn left by someone who perhaps went to the bathroom. B uses the opportunity of the interruption to take the popcorn, as she is starving. B returns to the movie but feels badly about being rude to A and isn't sure what to do next.

Conclusion

The key to learning how to say lines on stage is contained in the unit breakdown. Through the creation of units of action (segments of the text divided into a series of goals for the character) the actor draws a map of behavior that guides how the role will be played. By determining the components of the units of action, the character's want or need (objective), how he tries to achieve that want (action), and what stands in his way (obstacle), the actor can focus on achieving a goal rather than trying to deliver lines in a specific way.

Chapter Eight: From Rehearsal to Performance

You now have the tools you need to begin creating a role from a play. You've spent time getting to know your body, your voice and your imagination — the tools you will use on stage to communicate your intent. You've learned how to read a play and understanding its structure and central problem. You know how to find the given circumstances that directly affect your character. You can break a scene down into units of action with appropriate objectives, actions, and obstacles and perform them for your classmates. It's time to put all those skills together in the rehearsal and presentation of a final scene. Here are some tips to assist you in the process.

A. How to Rehearse

Good rehearsal is an important part of a successful performance. There are two key elements to a good rehearsal process.

1. **Make sure you rehearse enough.** Rehearse with your partner for one and one half to two hours for every minute of your scene. If your scene is five minutes in length, you should plan on a rehearsal schedule of seven to ten hours before you present your final performance. You won't rehearse all of those hours in one sitting. Spread your rehearsal time out over the course of the two to three weeks of final scene work. Plan to meet for one- to one-and-a-half-hour sessions. Meet for as long as you and your partner can keep your rehearsal energized and focused.
2. **Make Your Rehearsals Count.** Although rehearsal might seem like a nice time to get to know your partner, you need to spend most of your rehearsal time working on the scene. Feel free to spend some time during your first rehearsal getting to know your partner, but don't waste a lot of later rehearsal time on idle conversation. It is good to plan to spend the first few minutes of each rehearsal reviewing what you've accomplished and what your goals for this

session might be. Spend the last few moments talking with your partner about what you learned during that session. Spend the bulk of your rehearsal time playing the scene. Repetition is informative. If you are actively pursuing your objectives and listening and responding to what your partner gives you, you may discover new and interesting things about how to play the role. The more you repeat the scene, the better you will be during your final performance.

Rehearsals have a journey that follows a predictable pattern. First rehearsals are often a read-through/talk-through of the script. Last rehearsals are often done with costumes and perhaps makeup. Here's an overview of what your rehearsals might look like:

Rehearsal Map
(All rehearsals are **one** hour in length for a **five**-minute scene for a total of **eight** hours of rehearsal.)

Rehearsal 1
- Meet with partner and read through scene.
- Discuss the central problem of the play and how it affects the characters.
- Determine the given circumstances of the scene.
- Set up the environment and determine what furniture will be used and where it will reside in the setting.
- Make a list of possible props and costumes.
- Read through the scene again.

Homework on your own: Write down given circumstances and unit analysis.

Rehearsal 2
- Discuss what you learned doing the homework.
- Block the scene by running through it holding the script.
- Reread the objectives and see if the blocking fits these goals.
- Repeat blocking or redo blocking as necessary.
- Repeat two to three more times.
- Discuss what was accomplished.

Homework: Begin memorizing lines, bring in props.

Rehearsal 3

- Discuss how line memorization is going and goals for rehearsal.
- Run through scene.
- Discuss what is working and what needs help.
- Work specific moments.
- Run through scene multiple times.
- Discuss what is working and where you need help from instructor.

Homework: Finish memorizing lines.

(First Class Presentation)

Rehearsal 4

- Discuss notes from instructor on first presentation and goals for rehearsal.
- Begin work on instructor notes.
- Repeat scene multiple times.
- Discuss what you learned and what you need to work on.

Homework: Start thinking about costumes, work on lines.

Rehearsal 5

- Discuss goals for rehearsal.
- Work scene.
- Discuss what is working and what needs help, determine costume choices.

(Second Class Presentation)

Homework: Find costumes for next rehearsal.

Rehearsal 6

- Discuss instructor's notes and goals for rehearsal.
- Work scene with costumes.
- Discuss what is working and what needs help.

Homework: Read play again from start to finish

Rehearsal 7

- Discuss discoveries in rereading play and goals for rehearsal.
- Work scene with costumes.
- Discuss what is working and what needs help.

(Dress Rehearsal in Class)

Rehearsal 8

- Discuss instructor's notes and goals for rehearsal.
- Work scene with costumes.
- Discuss what is working and what needs help.

(Final Performance)

This map offers guidelines for planning your rehearsals. You can accomplish much in a short amount of time. Do not be fooled by knowing your lines. Learning your lines should occur early in the process and is only a technical accomplishment. The real acting begins once your lines are memorized and you can begin focusing on your objectives and your partner.

B. Memorizing Your Lines

The question most commonly asked of an actor by someone outside the profession is: "How did you learn all those lines?" Learning lines is not a magical process. Anyone can do it. There are many different methods you can use to get off book. Here are some suggestions:

Methods of Memorization

- **Repetition** is the best method for learning lines. The more times you say the scene, the more easily the lines will come to you. If you are rehearsing according the map suggested above, you will have plenty of repetition during which you can memorize your lines.
- **Work with a partner**. Recruit someone to go over your lines with you. It need not be your scene partner. It can be a friend or family member. Have them read your partner's lines and cue you for yours.
- **Use a tape recorder** and tape the other person's lines with enough space in between for you to say yours. Practice in the car, as you walk to class, in your room. A tape recorder allows you to be independent of the need for a line partner.
- **Use a ruler** to cover the other character's line as you move down the page. Some people are visual learners and actually memorize lines according to their location on the page. Try it and see if it works for you.
- **Walk through the movements** as you memorize. If you are a kinesthetic learner, you learn best by doing. Using your

body to recreate the scene as you memorize may make the process easier for you.

Be sure to memorize the play *exactly as written.* Playwrights don't appreciate actors reinventing the lines. Memorize your words precisely. Ask those who help you to correct you when you make a mistake so that you can get it right when you play the scene.

What to Do If You Forget

During the memorization process you will find that the first time you present the scene in front of an audience without the text, you will have lost some of your memorization. You thought you knew your lines when you were back in your room, even in private rehearsals with your partner, but now suddenly, in front of an audience, they seem to go out of your head. This is a normal part of the process. Nerves do funny things to your thinking. For this reason, there is a protocol for dealing with line loss while running a scene.

- **Call for a line.** When you are unsure if you will remember your lines during a class presentation, have one of your classmates hold the text of your scene and follow along as you play. If you forget what to say while playing the scene, pause for a moment without losing your focus and call out "Line!" The person holding the text can then feed you the line. You'll pick it up the line and keep going without interrupting the continuity of the scene. For this process to work smoothly, both you and your prompter must speak loudly and clearly to avoid having to repeat yourselves.
- **Ad lib.** If you forget during a performance, calling for a line is not an option. The audience should never see that you've forgotten what to say. When an actor forgets a line during a performance, she or her partner must ad lib (make up dialogue) until one or the other of them can remember the actual lines in the scene.

C. Working with Your Partner

Theatre is a team sport. You are always working in partnership with someone. Even if you are doing a one-person show, you have the stage manager, the designers, and the stage hands to assist you in presenting your piece. In scene work, you will be working with a partner. Learning to work effectively with your scene partner will do much to ensure the success of your final scene. Here's some advice for forming a solid working relationship:

Partnership Protocol

1. **Communicate** in a timely and effective manner. Return phone calls and e-mails promptly to set up or confirm rehearsals. Talk to each other about problems you encounter right away.
2. **Be courteous** of one another's time and energy. Show up to rehearsal and show up on time. In the professional theatre, an actor is expected to arrive at rehearsal no later than ten minutes before the rehearsal is scheduled to begin.
3. **Be respectful** of one another's feelings and personal space. Never say something critical or cruel to your partner. Never touch your partner or talk to your partner in an inappropriate manner. If your partner behaves inappropriately to you and you feel violated or in danger, inform your instructor immediately.
4. **Never suggest** how your partner should say or play a line. Focus on your character and your work. Remember that you are working as a team, and neither of you is in charge. It is important to be able to trust and support one another as you work on your scene.
5. **Offer to help** your partner. Ask them if there is anything you can do in the scene that will help them accomplish a certain goal or moment. Your partner may have nothing to request or may accomplish a breakthrough with a problem spot through a simple adjustment in your performance. Regardless, it fosters goodwill when you offer to help one another.
6. **Come prepared**. Do your homework and be ready to work on the things you've discovered. The energy you bring to rehearsal will determine how well it goes.
7. **Leave no trace**. Leave the rehearsal space in better condition than when you found it. Throw away that extra trash, move the chairs back to their original position, put your things away.

If you follow these seven simple rules, you should have a positive experience working with your scene partner.

D. The Performance: Things to Think About

You've spent three to four weeks working on your scene. You've read the play, analyzed the given circumstances and units of action, you've been rehearsing and rehearsing. It's now time for the final performance.

Dealing with Nerves

Guess what? Veteran actors who've been working on stage for thirty years still get nervous. Nerves are an important part of the energy of a performance. Being nervous is good. But you need to learn how to channel that nervous energy. Two things work well in converting nerves into positive playing energy.

1. **Practice**. Make sure you've practiced enough to feel confident in playing your scene. Practice is the most effective antidote to nerves. Those who are the most nervous have usually spent the least amount of time practicing the scene.
2. **Focus**. Focus on your partner, not on the audience. It's those people watching who are driving you crazy. Forget about them. Look at your partner, remember your first objective, and go after it. If you are really focusing on getting the character's needs met, you will be too busy to be nervous. Of course, feel free to employ the old standby and imagine the audience in their underwear. Whatever works to get your mind back on telling the character's story.

Take the Time to Set Up

You will be performing on a program with every other scene in class. Because final scene presentation time is often short, you will find yourself pressured to quickly set things up and then to go. Take a moment before you move into your place to begin the scene and make sure you have props set, the furniture is in the right place, and you have everything you need. Nothing will throw you more than discovering you forgot to set the wineglass you pick up and carry around in the scene.

Take a Moment Before You Begin

Preparation time before you begin to perform doesn't have to last for two minutes. Thirty seconds will probably do the trick. Take a second to breathe and get your mind into the scene before you begin to play. Interestingly enough, this moment of preparation helps the audience as well. They can settle in and focus on the story you are going to tell them.

<u>Don't Forget to Have Fun!</u>
If you've done your homework and you've taken your moment to prepare, then the stage is yours. Enjoy your time to shine. Acting is fun, and the audience enjoys watching actors who are having fun. Indulge yourself in the delight of telling your character's story.

Conclusion

Scene work gives you the opportunity to synthesize all the skills you've learned in class. You'll begin to develop your teamwork technique as you learn to solve problems with your scene partner. Scene work gives you a chance to begin learning how to apply your new skills to the creation of character through the trial and error of the rehearsal process. The effort you extend when creating your character and perfecting your scene has its own reward as you present your hard work before an appreciative and enthusiastic audience.

Conclusion

Anyone can learn to master her performance. The first step in controlling the impression you make and the message you send is becoming aware of how you are behaving. Once you develop this awareness, you can begin refining your acting skills to control your performance, both onstage and off. You can modify the use of your body to appear poised and confident. You can modulate your voice to charm, soothe, or command. When you understand why other people do what they do, you can adjust your response to their behavior to achieve your goals. Like a character in a play, you may find that you have something you want to achieve (your objective), that you employ many tactics to achieve that goal (your actions), and that you often encounter obstacles along the way — both inside yourself and in the world around you. Whether or not you continue learning about acting and studying theater, the skills you've explored in this book will assist you in many of your life pursuits. In a job interview, during a graduation speech, or when talking with a grieving friend, it is important to choose how you are perceived and how you might communicate your intent.

Works Consulted

Adler, Stella. The Technique of Acting. Toronto: Bantam Books. 1988.

Barker, Sarah and Harrigan, Peter. Introduction to Performance: Beginning the Creative Process of the Actor. Third Edition. Dubuque: Kendall/Hunt Publishing. 1997.

Barkworth, Peter. The Complete About Acting. London: Methuen Drama. 1991.

Barton, Robert. Acting Onstage and Off. Instructor's Edition. New York: Holt, Rinehart and Winston, Inc. 1989.

Benedetti, Robert. The Actor at Work. Sixth Edition. Englewood Cliffs, NJ: Prentice Hall, Inc. 1994.

Brestoff, Richard. The Great Acting Teachers and Their Methods. Lyme, NH: Smith and Krause. 1995.

Bruder, Melissa, et al. A Practical Handbook for the Actor. New York: Vintage Books. 1986.

Chekhov, Michael. To the Actor. New York: Harper & Row. 1953.

Cohen, Robert. Acting One. Fourth Edition. Boston: McGraw-Hill. 2002.

Crawford, Jerry L. Acting in Person and in Style. Fourth Edition. Dubuque, IA: Wm. C. Brown Publishers. 1991.

Felner, Mira. Free to Act: An Integrated Approach to Acting. Ft. Worth, TX: Holt, Rinehart and Winston, Inc. 1990.

Gronbeck-Tedesco, John L. Acting Through Exercises: A Synthesis of Classical and Contemporary Approaches. Mountain View, CA: Mayfield Publishing Company. 1992.

Hagen, Uta. Respect for Acting. New York: Wiley Publishing. 1973.

Hodge, Alison (editor). Twentieth Century Actor Training. London: Routledge. 2000.

Itkin, Bella and Aven, Richard C. Acting: Preparation, Practice, Performance. New York: HarperCollins College Publishers. 1994.

Lewis, Robert. Advice to the Players. New York: Theatre Communications Group. 1980.

Lewis, Robert. Method or Madness? New York: Samuel French, Inc. 1958.

Levin, Irina and Igor. The Stanislavski Secret. Colorado Springs, CO: Meriwether Publishing Ltd. 2002.

McGaw, Charles and Clark, Larry D. Acting Is Believing: A Basic Method. Fort Worth, TX: Harcourt Brace Jovanovich College Publishers. 1992.

Moss, Larry. The Intent to Live: Achieving Your True Potential As An Actor. New York: Bantam Books. 2005.

O'Neill, Rosary. The Actor's Checklist: Creating the Complete Character. Fort Worth, TX: Harcourt Brace Jovanovich College Publishers. 1992.

Owen, Mack. The Stages of Acting: A Practical Approach for Beginners. New York: HarperCollins College Publishers. 1993.

Spolin, Viola. Theater Games for the Classroom. Evanston, IL: Northwestern University Press. 1986.

Stanislavski, Constantin. Building a Character. Sixth Edition. London: Methuen. 1986.

Yakim, Mona. Creating a Character: A Physical Approach to Acting. New York: Backstage Books. 1990.